Original title:
The Great Search for Life's Missing Key

Copyright © 2025 Creative Arts Management OÜ
All rights reserved.

Author: Gabriel Kingsley
ISBN HARDBACK: 978-1-80566-255-6
ISBN PAPERBACK: 978-1-80566-550-2

The Forgotten Language of Existence

In the realm of socks and spoons,
I seek the words of absent tunes.
A rubber chicken's wise advice,
Squirrels teach me, oh so nice!

Lost coffee cups with laughter plead,
While mismatched buttons plant a seed.
Cats decipher the cosmic signs,
In the chorus of their feline whines.

Echoes of an Unsung Melody

A rubber band snaps, oh what a tune,
Whistles of silence under the moon.
Crickets chirp in a jazzy spree,
While the toaster hums a symphony.

Muffins dance on the kitchen floor,
As spoons and forks beg for an encore.
Bananas boast their rhythmic flair,
Echoes spin in the fragrant air.

Seeker of the Unwritten Path

With every step, a banana slip,
A hidden path on a citrus trip.
A coffee stain is my guiding star,
In the world of where the weird things are.

In search of crumbs of laughter's grace,
I trip through time, a silly race.
Paper airplanes fly through the quest,
Giggling hats declare the best!

The Map of Infinite Possibilities

A treasure map with doodles bold,
Leads to wonders yet untold.
A compass spins with a cheeky grin,
Pointing to chaos where giggles begin.

X marks the spot on a chocolate lake,
With marshmallow islands for goodness' sake!
Pandas in sunglasses hold the clues,
In this wacky world of silly views.

Fables of the Invisible Key

In a kingdom of quirks and many a jest,
A key was lost, or so claimed the pest.
A chicken, a cat, on a quest through the fog,
Debating the value of a lost old log.

They searched through the pantry and poked at the floor,
Found pickles and socks, but not much more.
The wise old owl chuckled from high in a tree,
"You won't find the key among brined gherkins, you see!"

Unraveling the Threads of Life

Life's puzzle's a tangle, each thread a delight,
The more that you pull, the messier the plight.
A babbling brook stole one sneaker and sock,
And the fish laughed so hard, they forgot to talk.

Each whispering breeze gave a clue to behold,
But instead told of tales of who's daring and bold.
With knitting needles crossed, they puzzled away,
Life's missing threads? Oh, what fun in dismay!

The Map to Hidden Realms

A map in hand, it promised much gold,
Yet all it revealed were some flowers so bold.
A squirrel named Nutty, with a hat too small,
Declared, "Follow me, I'll help you find it all!"

Through fields of wild pudding and rivers of jam,
He tripped on his shoelace and landed with splam.
The land of the lost was a comical sight,
With keys made of jelly that danced in the night.

Journeys Beyond the Ordinary

I ventured beyond where the people grow strange,
In lands where the clocks seemed quite out of range.
A llama named Larry, with a grin oh so wide,
Claimed he had secrets the sun couldn't hide.

We climbed up a mountain made of old cheese,
With every step higher, we laughed with great ease.
The key to my heart, he said with a glee,
Is just being silly, set your spirit free!

Through the Lens of Wonder

In a world of quirky quests,
I lost something, oh what a mess!
With a sock and a spoon, I begin,
Maybe it's hiding where laughs spin.

I asked a cat with a wise old stare,
It flicked its tail, said, 'Check under there!'
With a map made of doodles in hand,
I'm seeking my key in this silly land.

From talking trees that giggle and sway,
To roundabout routes where squirrels play,
Each twist and turn, a giggling chase,
For a key to a door, in a funny place.

Upon a cloud, I found a shoe,
But no key in sight—what to do?
With each new whim, I'm led astray,
In laughter and joy, I'll find the way.

Fragments of a Glorious Quest

I ventured out with a bright red hat,
To find what's lost, how about that?
With a sandwich, a dog, and maybe a tree,
I'll unravel this riddle, oh so merrily!

A wise old frog croaked, 'Jump this way!'
I leaped and twirled, what a ballet!
Searching high, searching low, full of cheer,
Forget the key, I found a beer!

Chasing shadows of clouds, what a sight,
With thunderous laughter, my heart took flight.
In this scrap of life, joy fills my quest,
Fragments of fun make the search the best.

With each odd item that I collect,
I'm piecing together this riddle, unchecked.
For the key might be laughter, or joy so true,
In the end, it seems, I'm just following through.

Keys Underneath the Surface

In the couch, where crumbs reside,
I searched for keys that used to hide.
Under cushions, lost and meek,
They laugh at me, the things I seek.

Unlocking doors to nowhere fast,
With every swipe, my patience passed.
Perhaps they're off, a grand old spree,
While I'm stuck here, searching for glee.

Canvases of Unexpressed Thoughts

On watercolor papers, ideas dance,
But every stroke seems just a chance.
My thoughts, like paint, get muddy there,
Beneath the surface, a blank stare.

A masterpiece waits in my mind,
Yet every brush leads to the blind.
So I scribble notes, all out of view,
While my deepest muse just laughs, 'Who knew?'

Cracks in the Fabric of Reality

Reality bends in quirky ways,
With creaks and cracks that start to play.
I peek through seams with hopeful eyes,
    Hoping to stumble on surprise!

A sock, a shoe, a rogue spaghetti,
Behind the curtain, life's confetti.
In all this mess, I find my theme,
    Reality's just one wild dream.

The Lost Riddles of Being

In the depths of my morning brew,
I search for riddles old and new.
Why do toasters always burn?
I ponder long, then take my turn.

A jigsaw puzzle without a piece,
Each question stabs, yet none bring peace.
The humor shines in every clash,
As I sip on hope and munch on hash.

In Pursuit of Life's Essence

I once misplaced my favorite shoe,
Where could it be? I haven't a clue.
The fridge's humming could be a sign,
A treasure map for my missing brine.

I search in drawers, I search in the yard,
Found some old socks and a half-eaten shard.
Yet all that remains is a dust bunny's face,
Laughing at me in this frantic chase.

The Treasure of Lost Moments

I lost my keys at a party last night,
Dancing with snacks, what a terrible plight.
I checked all the dips and the punch bowl, too,
Maybe they're sipping on soda with Lou?

The cat just laughed as I overturned chairs,
I offered him treats, he just gives me stares.
Life's little moments, they slip right on by,
Maybe my keys just decided to fly.

Journey Through the Veil of Time

I ventured back to my teenage years,
Searching for wisdom, all I found were fears.
A sparkly shirt and mismatched socks,
Reminders of dancing in plywood blocks.

The clock ticked loudly, mocking my quest,
While I pondered hard on the mundane jest.
But what if the key is my old mixtape?
With poorly drawn hearts and a psychedelic shape?

In Quest of What Remains

I'm off to find my youth in a jar,
A pickle, perhaps? Or a chocolate bar?
I searched high and low, through seasons and memes,
But all I found were some soggy old dreams.

I laughed at the chaos, my plan turned awry,
With ice cream cones flying, oh my, oh my!
Yet in all this madness, joy comes and goes,
As I trip over fun, where the wild laughter flows.

Reflections on a Shattered Mirror

Once I lost my car keys,
They vanished like my lunch.
Looked under the couch cushions,
Found a sock, very crunchy.

Thought they might be in my pants,
But all I found was lint and fluff.
Maybe they're out having fun,
Whirling with my missing stuff.

A mirror showed my puzzled face,
What's this? A chip in the glass!
I laughed, oh what a silly chase,
Next time I'll just buy a brass.

So here's to stolen moments,
And keys that love to roam.
In this wacky game of hide and seek,
I'll always chase them home.

Keys to the Soul's Repository

They say my soul's a treasure chest,
Locked tight with quirky keys.
Yet I've lost more than a dozen,
A real conundrum, if you please.

The first one was a rubber duck,
Bright yellow, oh so fine.
Now it guards the dusty closet,
Always ready to unwind.

I tripped over old shoelaces,
Found a musty old old hat.
What's that? My imagination?
Or just my grandma's favorite cat?

If my heart is truly hidden,
In this game, I'll surely win.
With giggles and some whimsy,
A journey set to begin!

Whispers on the Wind

I heard the wind whisper secrets,
About lost socks and feathered hats.
But when I chased those breezy tales,
I tripped right over my own mats.

A tree laughed as I stumbled past,
Swaying in wittiness so grand.
Maybe the key lies in that grin,
Of the wind's playful, teasing hand.

I asked the daisies for help,
They just swayed and said, 'No way!'
In the garden of lost ideas,
I might just plant a joke today.

So next time when I'm wandering,
I'll make sure to laugh and spin.
For the whispers might be leading me,
To the fun that lies within.

Tides of the Unseen

On the shore, I searched for treasures,
For a key that's lost in foam.
But all I found were clams and shells,
Not a key, just salty loam.

The waves chuckled with glee and cheer,
As they danced upon the sand.
They knew my quest was quite absurd,
And I was merely their brand.

I attempted to negotiate,
With the seagulls overhead.
'Can you lend me some insight here?'
But they just cawed and fled.

Now I sit with a sandy grin,
Watching the surf roll by.
Maybe lost things hold the secret,
To laughter and a joyful sigh.

In Pursuit of the Untold Story

I lost my keys in a pancake stack,
Flipped them high, now they won't come back.
Searching under cushions, what a sight!
Cats laugh at me, oh, what a plight!

I asked the dog if he'd seen the shine,
He just wagged his tail, said, "It's fine!"
Maybe a squirrel took them for a spin,
Or hid them away with a cheeky grin!

My buddy claims he saw them fly,
In a hot air balloon, way up in the sky.
Should I go check or just stay here?
Fried eggs and laughter fill the atmosphere!

So on I wander in this silly chase,
With crumbs in my pockets and a smile on my face.
Maybe one day I'll find that ring,
But for now, I'll dance and laugh, let's sing!

Fragmented Reflections of a Dream

In dreams, I find my lost laundry sock,
Dancing with shirts in a magical block.
The dryer hums tunes of a time long past,
Where mismatched pairs were a holdover cast.

I tiptoe on clouds made of fluff and foam,
Forever searching for a stylish home.
The clock strikes twelve, and I start to slip,
Down a rainbow path—watch your grip!

I stumble on turtles who wear tiny hats,
Sharing secrets of the world's missing spats.
We laugh, we sing, oh, such splendid fun,
But still, I need that sock, or my dance is done!

So here I stand, in this whimsical place,
With laundry on my mind, a fabled race.
Maybe tomorrow, in the light of dawn,
I'll find that sock and then I'll yawn.

The Enigma of Existence

What is the meaning behind my lost shoe?
Did it wander off, or did I bid it adieu?
I question the universe, stars shining bright,
As I trip on my laces in a comical plight.

In coffee shops, I seek clues in my cup,
Playfully stirring, never wanting to give up.
Baristas chuckle, they know what I'm at,
Hunting for answers while sipping on that.

The squirrels debate, their opinions are loud,
On the meaning of life—what makes them so proud?
I toss them a cracker, they gather around,
We ponder big thoughts, while munching on ground.

Laughing at riddles the world hands me here,
I muster my courage, push aside my fear.
With a wink to the cosmos, I carry on bold,
For with every mishap, new stories unfold.

Gathering the Pieces of Us

We searched for the puzzle, each corner and edge,
Found a piece in the fridge, under the hedge.
Laughter erupted as friends joined the quest,
For assembling this jigsaw, we're simply the best!

Armed with snacks and a goofy old map,
We stapled our hearts to the search in a snap.
Jigsaws and giggles, we mix up the parts,
All missing pieces, just chips of our hearts.

A chicken shows up with a feathered flair,
Clucking directions, we stop and we stare.
With each twist and turn, joy fills the air,
As we gather our memories—beyond compare!

At last, we find it with a computer mouse,
Nestled in tales, in our wayward house.
So here's to the ride, the fun and the fuss,
For in every lost piece, there's a part of us.

In Search of the Forgotten Door

In the attic, dust and dust,
I found a key that looked like rust.
It fit in a lock, but oh, surprise!
It led to a cupboard filled with pies!

The door it opens, a nutty place,
With dancing squirrels and a smiling face.
They served me tea with extra cream,
And asked me if I wanted a meme!

I wandered through halls of jam and bread,
With rhymes in the air that tickled my head.
A missing key, so very grand,
Unlocking laughter with a magic hand!

Echoes of What Once Was

In a garden where shadows play,
I heard a whisper, 'Come this way!'
It spoke of treasures, old and bold,
But all I found were shoes of gold!

They danced around with a silly beat,
Wiggling toes and twinkling feet.
An echo called, but what did it say?
'Check the fridge for yesterday's play!'

A fridge of giggles, a snack of glee,
Where pickles wear hats as silly as me.
I laughed so hard, forgot my key,
In a world where fun is the real decree!

Wandering Through the Labyrinth of Being

In a maze of thoughts, I lost my way,
It twisted and turned both night and day.
A signpost read, 'Please don't look down!'
But I saw a cat wearing a crown!

'Oh dear, oh me, lost and confused!'
The cat just grinned, a little amused.
He offered me tea brewed with glee,
And asked if I wanted to fly, like a bee!

Through tunnels made of dreams and cheers,
I followed the trail of a thousand fears.
But every turn brought silly sights,
With giggling giants and playful knights!

The Truth Behind the Curtain

Behind the curtain, what's the fuss?
A hamster wearing a purple bus!
He waved me in with a friendly grin,
'Welcome to the show, let's begin!'

The stage was set with pies that dance,
And dreams that twirled, given a chance.
I searched for truth, but found some play,
With jokes and laughter leading the way!

The truth, it seems, is not what it seems,
It lives in the laughter and silly dreams.
So here's a key that unlocks the fun,
A life of joy has just begun!

Isles of Forgotten Possibilities

In a land where socks go missing,
And keys play hide and seek,
There's a treasure map unrolling,
With clues as vague as a sneeze.

The fridge hums a secret song,
Of delights long gone astray,
While dust bunnies laugh at us,
As we search for yesterday.

Pineapple on pizza reveals,
More than appetite or fight,
It's the quirks of life's puzzle,
That spark joy in the night.

Yet all we find are cat toys,
And a sandwich made of air,
But we smile at each oddity,
For laughter's everywhere.

The Silent Symphony of Life.

Life plays a tune without notes,
Its rhythm like a wobbly bike,
Chasing after invisible ghosts,
In a quest for what we like.

A dog in a tutu pirouettes,
While pigeons plot their next move,
As we sip coffee meant for sleep,
And groove to our own grooves.

Lemons in the oddest places,
And jellybeans that tell no lie,
All enthroned in our mishaps,
As we wonder, oh me, oh my!

The symphony hums on forward,
With harmonies left to prank,
For life's a stage of laughter,
Where we play both saint and crank.

Unlocking Shadows

In the attic where dreams get tangled,
And memories wear funny hats,
We fumble with clocks, doors, and locks,
Searching for moments that never sat.

Dust motes dance like fairies,
Amidst the clutter of our past,
Each lock unhinges a riddle,
That leaves us bewildered and fast.

We chase the end of a rainbow,
While wrestling with a pet cat,
For shadows whisper the oddest tales,
That make us want to laugh and chat.

Each discovery is a patchwork,
Of life's most curious play,
Unlocking laughter from silence,
As we chase the night away.

Quest for Hidden Echoes

In the garden where secrets lurk,
Amongst the weeds and sun,
We search for echoes of laughter,
Where the weird and wacky run.

A frog wearing glasses croaks aloud,
As butterflies write poetry,
In the symphony of plants and stones,
Life's humor is plain to see.

Old teapots spill tales of yore,
While gnome statues strike a pose,
Our adventure splashes in color,
With antics that nobody knows.

So here's to quests of odd wonders,
In gardens of untold cheer,
For every echo we uncover,
Brings laughter ever near.

A Tapestry of Lost Hopes

I misplaced my joy on a shelf,
Hoping it'd mingle with my other self.
It rolled into the kitchen, I can't believe,
Next to the cookies, trying to weave.

I checked the sock drawer, it wasn't there,
A game of hide and seek, like life's unfair.
With every step, I trip on a shoe,
Wondering what else I might just misconstrue.

So I laughed at the chaos my life tends to sprout,
Is life just a game where we always shout?
With laughter as glue, I stitch on anew,
Collecting lost keys, who knew they grew?

Ah, this tapestry of hopes gone astray,
We'll dance through the mess, come join the ballet!
We'll find that lost laughter beneath our feet,
And spin it all into a whimsical treat.

The Hidden Architecture of Life

I often build castles from dough and dreams,
But they always collapse, no matter how it seems.
One day it's a fortress; the next, a pie,
Just roll with the punchlines, give that a try!

I found plans for a mansion in yesterday's news,
Laced with spaghetti? Well, that's just my muse.
Blueprints in crayon, what a sight to be seen,
Constructing a life that's quite more than routine.

With each bizarre structure I try to erect,
My neighbors all giggle, I hope to collect.
A prize for the oddest design that I make,
Something unique, like a life full of cake!

So here's to the blueprints that twist and deform,
In the architecture of laughter, we weather the storm.
Let humor be banter, a giggle or two,
In this wild realm of life, it's a glorious view.

The Quest Beyond the Surface

Digging deep in the couch for lost coins,
Finding strange relics, like old, chewed-up loins.
There's treasure galore beneath cushions, I swear,
An intergalactic quest, without a care!

I've encountered a pencil, my long-lost friend,
It's been hiding for ages; it's time to mend.
With crumbs and old tickets, what luck I perceived,
A circus of magic, a mess I believe!

With every small trinket, a story unfolds,
Like searching for diamonds in mountains of gold.
The more that I dig, the more I unearth,
A comedy show that defines my true worth.

So here is my motto, oh seeker of dreams,
Life can be bonkers—more fun than it seems!
Grab your magnifying glass, join in the spree,
Let's treasure the silliness, just you and me!

Awakenings in the Stillness

In stillness, I ponder my slippers' great plight,
Why do they vanish in the dark of the night?
A sock may escape, but a shoe has a plan,
To roam on the floor like a rebellious man!

I sit in my chair with a cup and a sigh,
The cat's on an adventure, oh my, oh my!
With each little tiptoe, I know what it means,
It's life playing tag, while I sip my routines.

Thoughts bubble up like popcorn in a pan,
In the quiet, they pop—what a zany clan!
A chorus of chuckles from nowhere they spring,
Awakening laughter—let the silliness sing.

So here's to the moments of stillness I dread,
When socks come alive and dance in my head.
With giggles as fuel, we'll embrace the delight,
In these silly awakenings, everything's bright!

Beneath the Layers of Time

In the attic, I found some socks,
Buried beneath a pile of clocks.
What treasure awaits behind old stains?
Perhaps a secret hidden in the chains.

A sandwich lost from '93,
Could that be the key to set me free?
With crumbs that whisper tales of yore,
Maybe lunch is what I'm searching for!

Clues in the Dust

Dust bunnies dance in the dim light,
If they could talk, oh what a sight!
They've seen the world while under the bed,
Some say they carry wisdom instead.

I asked a crumb, it just replied,
"Investigate! Come along for the ride!"
Together we ventured to find some clues,
But it just led me to yesterday's news.

The Pathway to What Is

In my garden, I lost a shoe,
What could it mean? Could it be true?
Is a missing flip-flop a sign from fate?
Should I seek it out while it's still late?

A worm waved at me from under a stone,
Could that be the key I should have known?
I followed it down a marshy trail,
Only to discover it was just a snail.

Fragments of the Infinite

Leftovers from the cosmic feast,
What happened to the ultimate beast?
A half-eaten cake from outer space,
Locked in the fridge without a trace.

I opened the box with a hopeful grin,
To find a moldy tupperware within.
Maybe the key was actually pie,
Or just a slice that said goodbye!

Where Secrets Dwell

In the closet where old shoes lie,
A sock sings songs, oh my oh my!
The cat tells tales of ancient days,
While dust bunnies dance in silly ways.

A search for treasures, lost and found,
In cereal boxes, secrets abound.
The fridge hums softly, 'What's your need?'
Perhaps a snack, or a tiny steed?

Chasing Whispers of Existence

Behind the couch, a crumb may speak,
Of hidden lives and snacks so meek.
The TV remote, where could it be?
Maybe it's off on a wild spree!

The goldfish gossips, bubbles rise,
Of missed adventures in disguise.
We laugh and search, what could we win?
A pair of pants, or a plastic din?

The Key Beneath the Stars

Under the moon, I look for signs,
A napping squirrel resists my lines.
Stars wink down with a twinkling grin,
As I trip over shoes that I've been in.

A map made of dreams, where could it lead?
To buried treasure, or just a weed?
With laughter echoing as I roam,
Will I find a key, or just my comb?

Searching for Forgotten Paths

In overgrown gardens, laughter swells,
With gnomes and faeries casting spells.
Through tangled weeds, I stumble and fall,
Crying out, "Is there treasure at all?"

A rubber chicken clucks with glee,
As I question my own sanity.
For every step in this wild dance,
Is filled with joy and second chance!

Whispers of the Unexplained

In a world where socks go to hide,
Celestial beings laugh and abide.
Where's the key to this messy fate?
I suspect it's lost with my lunch date.

The fridge hums a tune of despair,
With leftovers claiming they once were rare.
Mysterious echoes fill the night,
Did my sandwich just take flight?

Cats all gather to plot in the dark,
Training for their historic next park.
With every meow, a secret is spun,
Is the answer sirloin, or just plain fun?

So raise your glass to the quirks of life,
To hidden talent, and everyday strife.
For in jest and laughter, we may just find,
The missing key is to play and unwind!

Finding Clarity in Chaos

In the chaos of socks all mismatched,
My brain spins wildly, ideas dispatched.
Are they hiding from me in a grand masquerade?
Or is my cat the mastermind of this charade?

Coffee spills like wisdom, oh so rich,
From the cup to my notes, what a sketchy pitch!
I scribble notes on the back of my hand,
Do I even remember — or understand?

Puzzles missing pieces laid flat on the floor,
Needless to say, I've lost some before.
But in each challenge's peculiar strife,
Perhaps the joy's in the chase of this life!

So I wear mismatched shoes, feeling quite bold,
Embracing the chaos, in stories retold.
With laughter and drollness, a whimsical spree,
Maybe the key is just to let it be!

The Silent Call of the Unknown

In a closet, dust bunnies conspire,
To hide all the shoes that I truly desire.
Pair them or not, it becomes quite a game,
Oh, how I suspect that they feel no shame!

Books I've never read stack up like a wall,
"Just one more," I think, as they laugh at my call.
Each unopened page a world yet to guess,
But can I find out without causing distress?

With spoons in the drawer, where's the fork gone?
I suspect it went out for an early dawn.
Did it join forces with my missing key?
Or are they out hunting for brunch—just the three?

So I dance with my snacks and throw caution away,
For I might find treasures in a comical way.
The unknown whispers jokes with every sigh,
The missing key may just want us to fly!

Seeking the Light Within Darkness

In the depths of my fridge, there's a light so dim,
It flickers like chances that seem oh so slim.
A search for the snacks turns into a quest,
Why's the yogurt in hiding? This is quite the jest!

Shadows of laundry dance 'round my feet,
While monsters of socks throw a sock puppet meet.
Together they scheme with a mischievous laugh,
"Find the lost key, or will you take the path?"

In the corners of night, where the dust bunnies creep,
I stumble and fumble; oh, take a leap!
For in darkness and chaos, the truth may just gleam,
The key is a joke in the light of a dream.

So I chuckle and ponder, sipping my tea,
As I search through this maze, oh woe is me!
But with laughter, my heart grows ever so wide,
The missing key's here, just enjoying the ride!

Unlocking the Heart's Enigma

In a pocket of dreams, I found a shoe,
It asked for a dance, but I had no clue.
I laughed at the socks that had wandered astray,
While looking for love on a Sunday ballet.

A key made of chocolate, it melted away,
It sweetened my hopes but led me astray.
The lock on my heart squeaked like a rusty door,
As I fumbled for answers, slipping on the floor.

I chased after shadows that giggled in glee,
Searching for secrets in the cups of my tea.
With each sip of laughter, bubbles rose high,
I found all the keys were just pie in the sky.

But in every wrong turn, joy sprouted anew,
Each misstep I took joined the dance with a crew.
So here's to the journey, don't stare at your feet,
For the heart knows the rhythm, it's time to repeat.

Quest for Hidden Whispers

In a world where the gnomes are quite good at chess,
I ventured to find what would give my heart rest.
A map with a bop on a funky old beat,
Led me to whispers of laughter so sweet.

With a riddle, a pickle, and gum on my shoe,
I asked for directions from a wise kangaroo.
He danced in a circle, said, "Follow my tail!"
So off I went, with a whimsical sail.

I tripped over kittens, and they giggled with glee,
Each meow was a clue, but they wouldn't agree.
Keys made of marshmallows flew by like the breeze,
As I dodged all the whispers that teetered on knees.

At last, I found laughter tucked under a bed,
A treasure of giggles, where secrets were fed.
The key to my quest was not clever or sly,
It was just a big smile and a wink from the sky.

Pursuit of the Lost Secret

Around the old fountain, I danced with a sprout,
It giggled and whispered, then turned about.
I asked, "Oh dear sprout, have you seen my last key?"
It winked and it twirled, and it shouted with glee.

Through mazes of puzzles, I stumbled and chuckled,
With rubbery chickens, my brain gently buckled.
The search had become such a wacky parade,
We laughed till we cried as the sun slowly fade.

I gave chase to a snail, it promised a clue,
But all that it gave was a gooey review.
Each twist and each turn led me deeper in jest,
And I mused, "Perhaps laughter is the very best quest!"

So if you're dejected and searching with care,
Just trip over joy — it's floating in the air.
The secret is silly; it's not simply gold,
It's the giggles you gather as tales are retold.

Echoes of Unspoken Truths

In caverns of giggles where shadows like to play,
I searched for the truths that had wandered away.
With each silly echo, I burst out in cheer,
As whispers of wisdom tickled my ear.

A jester appeared in a hat made of cheese,
Declared, "All your answers are hidden in these!"
I rolled on the ground, laughter bursting like foam,
Who knew that the search could feel so much like home?

With each riddle unraveled, the day took its bend,
I realized the mystery found joy as a friend.
The truths that I sought were no grand masterpiece,
But silly confessions that never would cease.

So listen for echoes, they're neighbors of fun,
In every wild chase, the laughter's begun.
The missing key's here, no need for a map,
Just dance with your heart, wear a smile like a cap.

The Search for What Was Once Lost

I lost my keys beneath the couch,
They tumbled down with a little slouch.
I searched in every nook and cranny,
Once a simple task, now it's quite uncanny.

The cat just stared as I did dive,
Under the cushions, I tried to revive.
Finding socks from last year's wear,
But my missing keys? They're just not there!

I checked the fridge, maybe they were cold?
Among the pickles, brave and bold.
With every corner, the saga grew,
A quest for steel that feels overdue.

At last, I found them in my shoe,
Why they went there, I never knew.
Life's little mysteries often tease,
Keys in shoes, what a quirky breeze!

Dreamscapes and Distant Lands

In a dream, I lost my sanity,
Chasing clouds with a dash of vanity.
The moon wore shades, twinkling bright,
While stars threw parties all night.

My backpack held a rubber duck,
Who quacked advice, but just my luck.
Each step I took found me astray,
In lands where socks just fade away.

A dragon rode a unicycle,
Singing songs all night with style.
We spun in circles, laughing loud,
In this odd dream, I felt quite proud.

But when I woke, the pillow sighed,
And all my friends in dreams had died.
Yet, in my heart, their joy remains,
We'll ride again, through moony plains!

Guardians of the Hidden Gate

At the gate stood a grumpy troll,
With a beard that looked as if it rolled.
He demanded riddles, sharp and sly,
But would giggle if you said goodbye.

I asked him once, "What's your quest?"
"To guard this gate, it's quite a test!"
He laughed so hard, he dropped his sword,
Saying, "Look for laughter, not a reward!"

Behind the gate, a carnival lay,
With dancing bears and a bright buffet.
The troll joined in, a twirl and glide,
A friendly gatekeeper, full of pride.

In every riddle, he spread delight,
A tickle of joy in the starry night.
Life's hidden treasures, often found,
Are guarded by laughter that knows no bound!

Beyond the Horizon of Knowing

I sailed beyond the seas of thought,
Chasing replies that I never caught.
The fish wore hats and danced all day,
While jellybeans floated in the bay.

Flags waved with the wisdom of cheese,
As I asked the trees, "What do you please?"
They whispered secrets, soft and sweet,
But all I heard was, "Don't be discreet!"

With every wave, a giggle soared,
And every cloud was nicely ignored.
A parade of puzzling views did bloom,
In this land where nonsense found room.

At sunset's glow, I knew for sure,
In searching for answers, I'd find a cure.
For laughter brightens the darkest days,
And keeps the doubts forever at bay!

The Hunt for Forgotten Dreams

In a closet where hopes often hide,
I found a sock and a tattered guide.
Dreams so dusty, they forgot their names,
Playing hide and seek in the world's silly games.

Footprints of wishes in the sand,
Chasing shadows, isn't life just grand?
With a map made of chocolate, I venture forth,
To find those dreams and prove their worth.

A rubber chicken and a long-lost hat,
They say my fortune's stuck in this chat.
If I had a dime for every thought,
I'd buy back the dreams that life forgot.

So I gather my crew, a motley bunch,
Together we'll find that elusive hunch.
With laughter and glee, we roam and we play,
In the land of the dreams that never fade away.

Veins of the Universe

Stardust trails and coffee stains,
We reach for the cosmos while forgetting our gains.
With a slingshot made of whimsy and fun,
We'll bounce through the galaxies, one by one.

Planets spinning like a disco ball,
Who knew space was this much of a free-for-all?
Searching for answers in a cosmic stew,
Or maybe a burger, I'll take that too!

A jellybean comet zooms by with cheer,
While alien dancers all gather near.
"Show us your moves!" they giggled and spun,
We danced like fools—oh what fun we'd won!

In veins of the universe, laughter flows wide,
With each cosmic joke, we take in our stride.
So here's to the search, let it never be dull,
For life's truest joy is found in the lull.

Threads of Discovery

With yarns of knowledge, we weave our fate,
Creating a tapestry, isn't it great?
A stitch here, a seam there, oh what a sight,
Flying through thoughts in colors so bright.

But wait, is that a cat? Pouncing with glee!
Unraveling mysteries just to tease me.
Thread by thread, our journey unfolds,
With laughter as currency, the best kind of gold.

From fables of yore to puns of today,
Each strand tells a story in its own quirky way.
So we tangle and tussle, a raucous delight,
In threads of discovery, we take flight!

So bring on the fabric, let's fashion our dreams,
Sewing together our hopes at the seams.
For in every mishap and tangled way,
We find little treasures that brighten our day.

Unlocking Doors to Tomorrow

With a key made of laughter, I twist and I turn,
Unlocking the futures for which we yearn.
Each door holds a riddle, each handle a jest,
What's behind this one? Oh, let's take a quest!

A room full of jelly and dancing pink chairs,
Where socks with a passion perform in pairs.
Each unlock brings surprises, too wild to describe,
Like talking scarecrows who love to imbibe!

We stumble like toddlers on paths made of bliss,
With each fumbled step, we're led to a kiss.
The kiss of tomorrow, bold and surreal,
Where whimsy and wonder become part of the meal.

So here's to the doors we've yet to explore,
With a cheeky grin, let's open some more!
For with every lock that we dare to release,
We find the real magic and discover our peace.

A Voyage into Uncharted Waters

We set sail on a rubber boat,
With snacks and drinks, and hope to gloat.
The map's just scribbles, our compass broke,
Yet laughter echoes, a comical joke.

We searched the waves for a hidden treasure,
Each wave a billow, a sunlit measure.
A seagull stole my sandwich, you see,
Oh, what a journey, just you and me!

The fish were laughing, or so it seemed,\nAt our wild antics, we dreamily schemed.
We'd claim the prize of a bottle of rum,
Only to find out, it was just bubblegum.

At dusk, we spied a glowing light,
Turned out a lighthouse was our plight!
Yet returning home, with tales to spin,
We'll tell of the map, but it's all in the grin.

Discovering the Silent Threads

In search of something, a grand design,
I tripped on a thread, oh, how it entwined!
It led to a sock, mismatched and blue,
Where did it come from? I'd like to pursue!

My kitten was wiser, pounced like a king,
Chased all my worries, a plushy spring.
We followed the yarn, into the night,
Finding old treasures, a pure delight.

A spaghetti monster? Oh, never imagined,
In a world gone wacky, I felt so outlandish.
With each tangled mess, our giggles grew loud,
A search for the truth, in a yarn-spinning crowd.

In the end, we found, with soft smirks and grace,
Not all was lost in this chaotic chase,
For life's little joys, though puzzling they seem,
Are tied with a thread, like a silly dream.

Keys to Unlocking Tomorrow

I found a key, rusty and strange,
Promised to open a door full of change.
But where's the lock? I searched high and low,
Turns out it's hidden, like a secret show.

With every attempt, I twisted and turned,
The key loved the laughter, as I nearly burned.
Coconut juice spilled all over my shoes,
It seemed that today, there were just too many blues!

I thought of my neighbor, a man full of lore,
He said that the answer lies in a trapdoor.
I peeked through the bushes, saw shadows at play,
Found out they were kids, just playing all day.

So I laughed at the quest, what a twist in the tale,
The key, it exists, but not in a mail.
For tomorrow awaits with giggles in store,
Unlocking the joy that we all can explore.

Reverberations of Forgotten Truths

In dusty corners, I found a book,
Full of old tales, and a hidden nook.
It whispered secrets, in a comical tone,
The truth was silly, like a dog with a bone.

Forgotten wisdom, oh, what a find,
"Eat dessert first!" said the voice in my mind.
A salad of laughter, a banquet of cheer,
Dancing with shadows, a wild cavalier.

Each page turned over, a riddle or jest,
"Just find the punchline, and you'll feel blessed."
So I guffawed loudly, the walls shook with glee,
Life's grandest lessons, not so serious, you see.

And at the end, with a wink and a smile,
I closed the book, feeling light for a while.
For truth, when forgotten, can still be so bright,
Just find the humor, and you'll be alright.

Tales from the Abyss

In the depths where shadows play,
A fish wore glasses, swam astray.
He searched for treasure, found a shoe,
And chuckled, "What on earth to do?"

A crab with a map, quite absurd,
Had dreams of flying like a bird.
He hopped on a raft made of seaweed,
And shouted, "Adventure's what I need!"

Navigating the Map of the Heart

With a compass made of chocolate bars,
A squirrel set off to count the stars.
He drew a map with jelly beans,
And wondered where he'd find the means.

A wandering snail, oh what a sight,
Carried a balloon for his flight.
He floated past the old oak tree,
And said, "Is this where love might be?"

Searching for the Divine Note

A cat played piano with such flair,
The notes flew off to dance in air.
He searched for rhythms, looked in bags,
Then found a beat where laughter drags.

A dog joined in with a barking tune,
They sang all night beneath the moon.
A frog croaked loud, with joyful glee,
"Is this the music made for me?"

Whispers of the Unseen

In a forest where whispers swirl,
A gnome wore socks that made him twirl.
He danced with shadows, light as air,
And joked with trees that grew in pairs.

A fox with glasses peered for clues,
While sipping tea and sharing news.
"Have you seen my missing sock?" he said,
And laughed till he fell back, noggin red!

Reflections in a Broken Mirror

In a mirror cracked, I glimpse a face,
But it's just the cat, with a smug embrace.
Chasing shadows that giggle and tease,
Wondering where I left my car keys.

I rummage through drawers, a treasure hunt,
Finding old candy and a rubber stunt.
A sock puppet laughs, it has got no clue,
Is the key in the fridge, or maybe the loo?

The toaster chimed in with a witty retort,
'Check the garden; that's where things cavort!'
I'm starting to doubt my sane little quest,
Perhaps life's key is a good old jest.

So I dance with the broom, let the laughter flow,
For in this great quest, it's a comedy show.
Life's hidden treasures often go awry,
Maybe it's just to make us all sigh.

Cracking the Code of Existence

A riddle to solve, like where did it go?
The remote turns on—now that's quite a show!
I'll scribble some notes in a frantic spree,
Asking my goldfish if he's full of glee.

I tried Morse code with my spoons and forks,
But all they said was 'Eat more snacks, you dork!'
Mathematics confounds, it twists and bends,
Why can't my fruit salad just make amends?

In a world made of puzzles and extravagant schemes,
Could laughter itself be the missing themes?
Unraveling numbers, but it usually ends,
With my cat stealing socks and forming new trends.

So here's to the quirks in this life's little game,
Chasing the answers while avoiding the flame.
Each twist and each turn just make cocoa fun,
In cracking existence, we all are the pun.

The Hidden Compass Within

Found a compass that only points to lunch,
I'm lost in the woods, but there's soup to crunch.
With a map made of chocolate—don't ask where from—
I navigate snacks, it's a flavor bomb!

My GPS glitched, it leads to a cake,
Misreading my thoughts like a big, tasty fake.
But who needs directions in a world so wide,
When the best kind of journey is what's inside?

In pockets of wonder, I stumble and trip,
Following breadcrumbs, they lead to a dip.
The compass confuses, spins round and round,
But laughter's the key that's easily found.

So let's toast to our maps, our dishes divine,
To the hidden compasses that sparkles like wine!
In the heart of our folly, the treasures we seek,
Are the giggles and grins upon every peak.

Unraveling the Ties That Bind

My shoelaces entwined like a couple at prom,
In this dance of uncords, what's so wrong?
Each knot tells a story, a tangle profound,
While I'm tripping and laughing, falling all around.

Searching for purpose, like finding a sock,
One's missing its pair—what a terrible shock!
The laundry room chuckles, it knows all the tales,
Of socks that went rogue on windblown gales.

In this glorious mess of defined destiny,
I've misplaced my keys, join this rhapsody!
From the ties that we cherish, to jokes that we share,
The laughter we net is beyond any compare.

So here's to a life unwound and unfazed,
With ties we can crumble into endless displays.
The bindings are funny, all part of the grind,
In the chaos of living, what treasures we find!

Chasing Shadows of Existence

In the attic, I found a sock,
Maybe it holds life's biggest shock!
With crumbs and dust, it could unlock,
A mystery inside a sturdy box.

I checked my fridge, thought it was wise,
Could ketchup hold the ultimate prize?
Among cheese and pickles, I did surmise,
It's all a plot, or just my fries?

The cat stared hard at a wall of grey,
Perhaps it knows the key's today!
But all she did was lay and play,
Maybe that was the secret way?

So I dance with shadows at twilight's call,
Each step leads to a possible fall.
Yet I laugh and spin, enjoying it all,
For in the chase, there's joy to recall.

The Key Beneath the Surface

Beneath my bed, dust bunnies roam,
Maybe they're hiding the key to home.
I reached down low, gave them a comb,
Found an old sandwich—oh, how it's grown!

The bathtub whispered sweet secrets near,
Could the soap be an answer clear?
I scrubbed and splashed with silly cheer,
Found my rubber duck, just meant to leer.

The goldfish said with a bubble's rise,
"Life's keys are hid where humor lies."
I stared back blank, to my surprise,
The tank just giggled, no need for sighs!

A mop stood still, like a statue grand,
Did it know something I'd never planned?
With broom and dustpan, we made a band,
Creating music, just as we'd planned!

Searching for What Slumbers

In the garden, I found a snail,
Do you think it's dreaming of a great trail?
With a pop of its shell, it might unveil,
The truth behind this curious tale.

Under a mushroom, I took a peek,
An old gnome napped, his beard quite chic.
I poked him gently, he let out a squeak,
"Back off, my friend, I'm not at my peak!"

The squirrels held a council, plotting quite keen,
To determine just who was the best in cuisine.
But who knew they favored acorns pristine?
I joined their debate—for a moment, I'm seen!

As the sun sets, and shadows grow long,
I chase down laughter and sing a song.
For the key to life, where we all belong,
Is simply to join in and play along.

Mysteries Veiled in Silence

In a closet hidden, full of old ties,
I heard a whisper, or maybe a sigh?
'Twas my ex's sweater, a colorful lie,
Could it hold secrets? Oh me, oh my!

The toaster laughed when I dropped my bread,
"Search inside me, for dreams you've shed!"
But all it had was a crumply spread,
Still, I thanked it for making me fed.

A old lamp flickered, said "What's the fuss?
Your missing key is here, don't rush!"
I rubbed and rubbed, got lost in the hush,
And found dust bunnies in quite a crush!

In corners dim, where silence prevails,
I chuckled to think how life's odd tales,
Reveal the key in the quirkiest trails,
It's laughter and dance that always prevails.

Forgotten Pages of the Soul

In drawers of dust, I found some clues,
A rubber duck and slightly used shoes.
These pieces of me have gone astray,
Like socks in the wash, they've lost their way.

A map of crayons led me on a quest,
For peanut butter sandwiches, I must confess.
Chasing after memories, I nearly tripped,
On ice cream cones, I once brightly dipped.

Each laugh a note, each sigh a tune,
I danced with shadows under the moon.
Finding my heart on a cereal box,
Is like asking a fish to wear some socks.

So here I sit, with pages anew,
Reading the jokes, life's vast rendezvous.
If missing pieces I ever find,
I'll wear them proudly, sweetly entwined.

In Pursuit of Elusive Light

With a flashlight stuck in my bewildered grip,
I scoured the attic for a ready tip.
Chasing reflections on the walls so bright,
Wondering if I'd trip over sheer delight.

A cat named Whiskers gave me the glare,
As if to say, "That's not quite fair!"
He lounged in sunbeams, oh so smug,
While I danced with dust, feeling quite a thug.

I spun in circles, a tumbleweed wild,
Chasing my shadow like a lost child.
But just around dusk, I found my way,
In a jar of glitter from a far-off day.

The light I sought was hidden in fun,
Made of laughter and warmth from the sun.
So now I learn, with a joyous heart,
The chase itself is a curious art.

The Treasure of Being

With a treasure map drawn in crayon and dreams,
I set sail for riches, or so it seems.
An X marks the spot on my pizza slice,
Hope for gold coins in the land of nice.

Gummy bears, my trusty crew,
Stuck on the deck like candy glue.
A parrot named Popcorn squawked from the mast,
"Dig deep, my matey, this quest's a blast!"

Beneath the floorboards, I found a stash,
Old toys and trinkets, a whimsical bash.
No doubloons of silver or jewels so rare,
Just memories twinkling like fireflies in air.

So I hoisted my flag in this sugary sea,
Realizing the treasure was always with me.
Every laughter, a gem, every story, a ring,
Turning life's moments into bling for the spring.

Footprints in the Cosmic Sand

Across the universe, I took a stroll,
In flip-flops and giggles, feeling quite whole.
Footprints in stardust, a whimsical trace,
Dancing with aliens in outer space.

The stars were winking, playing a game,
While planets chuckled at my silly name.
A comet whizzed by, with a wink and a nod,
"Did you bring snacks?" was its cosmic plod.

The moon dropped a wink, "Join the parade,
Where laughter's the music, and joy's unmade."
I leaped on a cloud, feeling the breeze,
With a chorus of suns singing "Do as you please!"

These footprints I leave, so light, so bright,
Are echoes of laughter in cosmic delight.
For in every step, every giggle, I find,
The key to my heart intertwined with the mind.

www.ingramcontent.com/pod-product-compliance
Lightning Source LLC
Chambersburg PA
CBHW071825160426
43209CB00003B/210